SEASONS OF LOVE

SEASONS
OF LOVE

Donni Betts and George Betts

CELESTIAL ARTS
Millbrae, California

Celestial Arts
231 Adrian Road
Millbrae, California 94030

First Printing, April 1980

Made in the United States of America

Cover photograph by Don Corning
Cover design by Betsy Bruno
Interior design by Wendy Cunkle Calmenson

Library of Congress Cataloging in Publication Data
Betts, George, 1944-
    Seasons of love.

    I. Betts, Donni, joint author.   II. Title.
PS3552.E85S4   811'.54   79-55470
ISBN 0-89087-243-0

1 2 3 4 5 6 7 8 — 86 85 84 83 82 81

For Kristi and Jordi

In the springtime of our love
we sensed a newness, a freshness in the air,
      a sense of the birth of something
            that would change the course
      of both our lives.
Love blossomed, flourished, as it was
tenderly nurtured.

With summer came the intensity,
      the heat of conflict,
painful but necessary for the growth
      of any relationship,
as we struggled to understand each other
      and how we might join our two selves
and yet retain our independence.
As summer came to a close, the force
      of our conflicts lessened.

Autumn brought a new exhilaration,
the excitement that can come with the ending
of one season
      and the beginning of another.
More secure in our love we began to reach out,
      to make new friendships,
            to discover new and colorful dimensions
            we had overlooked in ourselves before.

Winter came to our love,
and we returned to the warmth
    and security of each other,
    comfortable in the knowledge
        that together,
    with patience and tolerance
we could weather any storm.
Our love has grown
    from openness, honesty
and devotion to each other
as well as our selves,
    and we are strong.

Spring has come again,
and with it
    the sense of newness,
as we continue to nurture
and cultivate the love
that blossomed long ago.
With each season,
    each year,
the roots of our love
    will deepen
and we will continue
    growing together. . .

SPRING

"Our love is the vehicle
that will carry us into tomorrow."

Several years have passed since we met. Our
lives have changed dramatically. We are stronger,
more secure with each other and more secure with
our selves. We have journeyed into unknown
lands, and back to the familiar, gaining insight
with each new step. I appreciate today, for we are
loving, in love and thoroughly involved with life.
We are fully alive . . .

But where did we begin? How did we get to this
place of acceptance and understanding?

I want to take time to understand our ever-
changing life, our ever-searching day-to-day living,
our belief in love, in life and in ourselves. I want to
look back, to reflect, to try to grasp an understand-
ing of the many seasons of our love . . .

It began with a look,
conveying a message
   we weren't yet ready
      to put into words.
Through our eyes,
   our expressions,
we began to form a language
of friendship,
a basis for the love we were
not yet ready to share.
Silently
our friendship grew,
our communication expanded.
Words gained new meaning
as the language of love evolved
and we became more sure of ourselves
in this new, exciting adventure.
And now, when we share a special look
I remember the first days,
   the days of that special friendship,
and I'm thankful.
For now, after all this time
     you are still my friend . . .

*Being alike
has brought us
together.
Being different
will help us
to grow.*

How can we be lovers
            if we aren't even friends?
Relationships develop so fast.
            Push — — no time for tomorrow.
Accomplish everything today
            but wait,
please slow down,
      let me show you
            what I am,
                  where I am, and
where I am going.

I want my freedom
              but I also want you.
              Can I have both?
              Are you different?
Will you give me new freedom to enjoy
Those things I would miss if you were gone?

Do I love you
  for what you are
  or what you give to me?
I hope it's just for
  what you are.
I'd like to think that
  you can be you
    and be free
      to go your way
      whenever you need,
that there's nothing here
  to hold you to me
  but the gentle breeze
    that moves softly
      between our souls,
    and speaks the things
      our words could never express . . .

My world
      and my heart
are open to you.
Be gentle,
take what you need,
      give what you can
for our time together
can enhance our lives.

I can not always be
  beautiful
    and unselfish.
You can not always be
  kind
    and understanding.
We are both human.
We have to be real.

Please be with me
when I cry,
when I'm down,
when I'm hurting.
I know it's hard for you,
that you get tired of it.
but that's what
loving is about . . .
sharing the hard times
as well as the good times.
I need you now
more than ever.
And you know
I'll be with you
when it's your turn to cry.

How wonderful to finally have found you.
For so long I searched,
looking for the special one
*   to share my life with,*
someone who would accept
*   and love me as I am,*
*   and yet provide the freedom and encouragement*
*   for me to outgrow my self-limitations.*
I longed for someone to admire, to love,
*   someone who was striving to be*
*   the best they could be.*
Yet somehow
*   each relationship fell short*
and I became more sure
there would never by anyone
*   with whom I could build a love*
*   and a life.*

Finally I stopped searching
and began to accept that
*   my life might be complete*
without having someone to share.
I began building friendships
*   rather than creating loves,*
and one of my friends
*   was you.*

Our admiration grew,
  nurtured by time
and love began to blossom,
    not from a need,
    but from a desire to be together.
And now,
    many years later
    I am thankful
we both stopped searching
and found each other. . .

The heart is not touched
continually,
but it is those precious times
that make everything
in our lives
worthwhile. . .

What was I like before I met you?

Was I growing, searching,
looking for answers through people
    and experiences?
Yes.
What am I like now that I have found you?
I am still growing, searching,
looking for answers through people
    and experiences. . .
How have you affected my life?
You have helped me to be
        more secure within myself,
            more aware of the feelings of others,
                more honest and spontaneous
                    in my experiences,
        more loving and accepting.
You have helped me to be more of what I am
    capable of becoming.
I have grown because of you,
        your love for me,
            and the security you have helped me to
            develop.
I am richer because of you. . .

SUMMER

*"To communicate with you
I must first know myself"*

We have achieved a unique balance in our relationship. You are strong, dynamic, outgoing. I am quiet, gentle, a listener. We both love people and when we are together our giving is multiplied by the balance in our personalities.

It has not always been easy. There has been conflict, struggle, as of course there must always be in a vital, changing, evolving relationship. But we see the difficult moments as opportunities for taking risks, for gaining a new understanding of ourselves and each other; a chance to go beyond our present circumstance.

We use our conflicts as an opportunity to communicate, and communication is the key to the balance in our life together.

What now?
We've talked for hours
but nothing has been said.

We care so deeply
but our feelings are lost
when we desperately try
to find each other.

You avoid my glances.
I talk about nothing. . .
Silence. . .
Finally the waiter announces
that it's time to close.

For moments our eyes meet
and I'm somewhat refreshed,
because even though it's painful
we'll try again.

Love is so hard to understand,
at times.

Frustration. . .
   incompletion. . .
Why?
   You helped create it
      and now you're asleep,
         safe,
and I feel alone
   What do I do with it?

I can't talk
   with no one to listen.
Maybe you're right. . .
   Maybe sleep is the answer
   for those who can. . .
      I can't.

You say you love me,
that you accept me,
But why do you frown when I act differently?
Can't you accept the different sides of me?
I must change as I live.
Don't ask me to sacrifice my growth
to meet your expectations.
I am what I am
If you do love me, you'll understand.

How can people
    who love each other
so much
    cause such hurt
        for each other?

Why do I say things
        that hurt you?
Why do you get
        so upset?
Why do we always
        have to withdraw?
Can't you see I'm
    willing to let go of
        the hurt feelings
and be close?

Don't you know that
    all I really want
        is to love you?

When I withdraw,
when I become defensive,
when I act as if I don't care.

These are the times I need you most.

If I hurt you,
it's not intentionally.
If you feel insecure with me
    it's not because I want it that way.
If I neglect to show you
how much I appreciate you,
    it's from a lack of awareness.
I try to do the best I can
but sometimes, in my bumbling,
        imperfect way,
I mess things up.
    Can you hear me?

Loving you is not always easy
  but if it were
    I probably wouldn't.

The time for honesty has come.

I can no longer hide behind
   excuses and avoidance.

I must finally accept the reality
   of my feelings
and face the consequences
   of owning them.

Because, painful as it may be,
   the truth
   hurts much less
      than trying to hide from it.

Admitting I was wrong
is the hardest thing I have done.
I was so sure of myself
and I knew I had
   to stand up to you.

But you were strong
   and now I understand. . .

Thank you for believing
    in yourself
  and for being
    honest with me. . .

I have grown. . .

To communicate with you
I must first know myself.
I must understand my needs,
my problems,
    my strengths and weaknesses.
I hear your words,
but not always your message.
My past gets in my way
    and I interpret what I hear
according to old experiences
even though they don't apply to
    our relationship.
I misunderstand you,
    and hurt follows.
I think you don't like part of me.
When will I be able to listen
    only to your message
    without putting a different meaning
        to your words?

I was angry with you
*   for changing,*
for not being what you've
*   always been,*
*   what I've needed you to be.*

I couldn't accept
that you were not the same
*   reliable person*
*   I've always counted on.*

I know we can't recapture
the past,
*   but can we go on,*
*   create something new*
from the change in our relationship?

It frightens me,
for I know it means that
*   I must change too.*
Is it worth it?
Am I willing to let go
*   of our old relationship,*
*   to build something new*
*   with what we now have?*

We're doing it once again. . .
solving our problems,
finishing our conflicts
and bringing closure to our lives.

Tomorrow
we might have
to begin once again,
but for today
we have brought peace
into our lives
and once again
we are able to relax
and appreciate what it means
to truly care. . .

I know you
almost
as well as
I know me.

I have learned
your moods,
your expressions,
your ability to give
and receive,
and the way you strive
to be. . .

Your past
holds both joy
and sorrow
and your future
is becoming
brighter
for you are developing
you.

I smile silently
as you continue to grow. . .

FALL

"What a wonderful task we have,
to work at living together,
keeping love alive. . ."

Our love has withstood the test of time and we are
coming to a new understanding of what
"together"can mean.

In the beginning I thought being together meant
sharing everything in our lives; that being apart
would mean losing some of the closeness we
treasure so much.

But as we have grown and become more secure,
both within ourselves and our relationship, we
have loosened our grasp and found that, through
time, it is the only way to hold on to something as
precious as our love.

"Together" can mean being secure enough in our
love to travel half-a-world away, alone. It can also
mean struggling with my self, knowing you will be
with me as I learn to resolve conflicts only I can
work through. Being together is knowing, finally,
that our relationship can survive many difficulties
and emerge stronger because we have learned once
again to work together, to listen, to understand.

It's Autumn again.
A year has passed
but the falling leaves
relive the memories
of our autumn.

We shared the
melting of the snow,
    the warming of the sun,
but then the leaves
    began to fall,
        and now I realize
that a tree must give
    and at times, become empty
before it is able to grow and give again,
and so it is with me.

At times I must leave you
and go deep inside
where I can explore
the mysteries of my mind,
of my being.

I must settle things
with myself . . .

then,
I am able to travel
back to you
and we can continue together
but at times,
I must leave you.

The time has come for introspection.
I need to look at my life,
    to find a direction.
Where am I going?
  What do I want my life
    to say about me?
The choices are mine.
My life will be what I make it.
There are so many directions.
The options are limitless.
I feel overwhelmed.
What if I make some wrong choices?

What if I do something I'll regret?
And yet I must remember
there is never any assurance
that life will be perfect.
But there is one thing
of which I can be certain . . .
I will always have ME.
My strength lies within,
and knowing that
is all the guarantee I will ever have
or truly need . . .

At times I need to wander
to distant lands and new experiences,
but life would not be complete
without the memory of home
and the ones I love.

I returned home today
and found our home
warm and alive.
I'm happy to be here with you.

In our relationship
we have discovered
how much we have to strive
    for our freedom . . .
not freedom from each other
    but freedom with each other,
to be what we truly are
        deep inside
and to know it's okay
    to be
        whatever that may be.

*Half of loving is
knowing when
to let go.*

Being far away from you,
I think of you often,
but it is not an empty feeling.
*   It is a feeling*
*   of appreciation.*
I remember the uniqueness
*   of your expressions,*
*   the depth*
*   of your loving,*
*   and the joy and laughter*
*   you bring to my world.*
And through my memories of you,
*   I am never alone.*

For as long as we've known each other
I've never really told you
how I feel about you,
    and I want you to know
what an important part of my life
        you are.

A friendship like ours
    is rare,
a chance for two people
    to share their everyday thoughts
        and deepest feelings
without feeling self-conscious
    or inadequate.

No matter how long
we've been apart
        my thoughts turn often
            to you,
and I smile,
knowing that the next time
I see you
        our friendship will have grown richer.

for we are both continually
        enriching our own lives,
bringing a new dimension
    to what we share.

The essence of me.
What does it mean?
How do I fit what I am
     with who you are?
How can we mold ourselves
into a twosome who can live together
     in harmony,
          striving for the same things . . .
Growth, happiness.
This must be the most difficult task in life . . .
to make a relationship work,
     to give it meaning, substance;
to find fulfillment together,
and yet manage, at the same time,
to develop the uniqueness of ourselves
          as individuals.
What a wonderful task we have,
to work at living together,
     keeping love alive . . .

Do you remember the
    "touching" moments
                of your life,
those small but significant times
that have helped you to be
    who you are now?
Last night I thought
    of the touching moments
and began to explore my past.

There was the excitement
    of being told
"You're beautiful, I love you."
There was the sorrow
    of saying goodbye
        to a true love
and knowing that love would never
        come my way again.
There was the sorrow of death
    and the search to understand.
There were the moments
    of being alone,
        when I began to learn
        about myself inside.

There was the feeling
of self-acceptance
and the excitement of reaching out
and finding others to love.

There was the satisfaction
of knowing that I am
changing and growing.
And now there is excitement
for today and
tomorrow . . .
I am open,
I am loved,
but most important,
I am alive.
My life has just begun . . .

WINTER

*"For now, after all this time,
you are still my friend . . ."*

Our love has changed. The newness is gone and
we are no longer living in a world of romance. Our
love will never be the same, but I feel no sadness
for our love has grown and we are stronger.
Although the newness is gone we now have a
deeper understanding, appreciation and respect for
each other as individuals.

Through our commitment we have developed the
security necessary to be ourselves, to take risks, to
be vulnerable.

We know the strengths, the weaknesses, the
goals and the dreams. We have experienced the
joys, the sorrows, the moments of anger and con-
flict, the times of tenderness and love. And through
it all we are renewed, ready for tomorrow, ready
to strengthen our love even beyond what it is to-
day. Our love has changed. . .

Do you still remember . . .
  The day we first met?
    The first time
      we shared silently?
  The first walk
      through the park?
  The awkwardness
          of opening up?
The first time we made love?
  The joy we shared
      as we discovered
  who we are,
          together?

So many things have faded from me
but not you, nor our memories.
They are so vivid,
          real,
as if they had happened yesterday.

Do you still remember . . .

It's funny . . .
people talk about falling in love.
But I didn't fall in love
                    with you.
I'm growing in love with you.

I brought you flowers today,
for the first time in many months.

Our pace has been so fast
that we haven't
taken time
    for ourselves.

We give so much to others.
Our world is rich and full.
We have built a world
    of security and love
with our friends and ourselves,
but through our journey
we haven't taken time
        for us . . .
And this is why I gave you
        flowers today,
a symbol of our love.

As you enjoy your gift,
take time to reflect.
These flowers represent
  our special moments.
Let us stop
  our involved pace
        if only for
moments,
  to take time
  to reflect,
    to appreciate,
  and to realize that
    we are living a love
  that many people
      only dream about . . .

Our love is self-renewing
for we provide ourselves
with new experiences,
        healthy friends,
exciting adventures
        and time to enjoy
the beauties and pleasures
of life.
We are not stagnant . . .
Our love is forever
        changing . . .

Funny, I never realized
how silent our home is
when you're away.

But even in the quiet
I feel
the comfort
of your presence.

Your gentleness will carry
me to sleep tonight
as it has every night.

Good night . . .
Sleep well . . .

You're sitting next to me,
half a world away,
        lost in your own thoughts . . .
I could feel lonely,
                left out,
            threatened.
But I don't.
I understand your need
            to be alone,
although we are together.
And this is the essence
            of our life together.
For at times
            we need to create
                a space
in which to reflect,
            to expand our thoughts
                in a way
which is impossible
if we cling too closely.
But no matter how far apart
        we travel
we remain together in our hearts.

Between
appointments,
people,
schedules
and deadlines
I have had
the time
to realize
how much
I love
and need you . . .
Tonight I'll bring
you flowers
and a bottle
of wine . . .
But before dinner,
please take
the phone
off the hook . . .

I find I hardly know this person
I've been living with for so long.
Lately we've grown,
    not apart,
        but in different directions.
I feel I don't know what happens
    in your daily life,
the forces that motivate you,
    the events that stir your emotions.
One thing I do know:
I find you intriguing
    exciting
        and most lovable.
A wonderful, vulnerable
and yet strong person.
I feel as though we're starting over,
    fresh,
        with renewed love
and interest in each other.

Nighttime,
Silence,
We are alone,
This time belongs to us
    as no other does.

Our bodies
    touching,
   our voices
    silent,
   our hearts
    together, peaceful,
For a few hours
the world consists
    of you and me.

Morning comes
and we slowly make our way
back into the world
of telephones
and other people.
But it's all right
because we always
have
our time,
The night belongs
to us.

For us,
love is more
than saying hello
            and later, goodbye.
Our love did not begin
            just to end.
We have built a love
        different from any
                we have ever experienced
                    before,
and the only thought
        we have about tomorrow
            is a continuation
                of today.

We have traveled
            through loneliness
            and sadness
to our place
        of understanding,
            our place of beauty
where we can continue
growing . . .
                together.

Why are we different from other couples?
So many relationships wither
but ours thrives on the sunshine,
 survives the storms
  and continues to grow
   stronger.

We are different
 for we have learned
  to let go,
   to communicate,
  to accept the differences,
to allow each other to be . . .

Our needs are being met.

I don't worry about tomorrow
 for we have learned to live today
to its fullest . . .

How fortunate we are to have each other . . .

We love each other,
        our love has
endured and has grown . . .
We will always face problems . . .
We will have conflicts,
                misunderstandings
and discomfort . . .

but we have the ability
to communicate,
        to strive for solutions,
to find new avenues of growth . . .

We love each other . . .
Our love is the vehicle
that will carry us into
                tomorrow . . .

I'm waiting
for spring to arrive.
For newness,
     green
          freshness
     to burst into our lives
and banish the heavy,
     cloud-days of winter.

Already I can feel
the sunshine
     brought by blooming
          daffodils.
     The first perfumed hint
     of new-mown grass
and the sense of endless freedom
     that warm, cloudless
          days promise.

The sun is hidden now
behind a blanket
     of heavy white flakes
and yet I feel
     the airiness of spring
          welling inside me,
          warming me already.
It won't be long now . . .